Teaching Scientific Enquiry

Contents

Introduction: *Teaching children about scientific enquiry*

When we ask young children to carry out science investigations we demand a lot from them. We ask them to:

- raise questions

- choose an appropriate approach

- plan what to do

- select equipment

- predict what might happen

- use equipment and carry out practical work

- make observations and take measurements

- present evidence in tables and charts

- draw conclusions and describe patterns and trends

- compare results with predictions and make further predictions

- suggest explanations.

We also ask them to use quite complex language structures, such as:

- asking questions 'How high will these balls bounce?'

- using the future tense 'I will drop them from the same height.'

- making comparisons 'This ball bounced higher than that ball.'

These are long lists of science and language skills, and we cannot expect young children to succeed in investigations unless we first break down these skills into small steps and then teach the children about each of them. If we do not take this approach, we end up either structuring the scientific enquiry so much that the children have very few decisions left to take; or we let them loose on activities for which they are not properly prepared, and they become overwhelmed.

How to use this book: *Questions and answers*

What will I find in the book?

There are 30 activities, called **Skill Activities**. It is difficult to teach younger infant children the skills they need to use out of context, as they need something in front of them to understand the point you are making. This book recognises this difficulty and so the **Skill Activities** are presented as either **Teaching strategies** or **Pupil activities**.

The **Teaching strategies** are techniques that suggest how to introduce scientific enquiry skills to children during 'on the carpet' discussion time. There are worked examples to show how things might happen in the classroom. The **Pupil activities**, which are presented on photocopiable worksheets, may be more suitable for older or higher attaining infant children.

All the **Skill Activities** are designed to improve children's knowledge and understanding of particular skills. This book places a high value on the conversations between teachers and young children and avoids suggesting that you should give inappropriate worksheets to the very young.

Should I do these Skill Activities instead of hands-on investigations?

The **Skill Activities** are not intended to replace hands-on scientific enquiries where children learn from first hand experience and direct observation. There can be no substitute for that. However, the **Teaching strategies** can help you highlight particular skills during a scientific enquiry, while the **Pupil activities** give children practice in using a skill before applying it to a scientific enquiry.

Which skills are taught in the book?

Eight skills are developed through various **Skill Activities**:

- asking questions and having ideas

- deciding on an approach

- planning what to do

- choosing equipment

- presenting evidence

- drawing conclusions and describing patterns in results

- comparing results to predictions and making further predictions

- explaining evidence.

All the skills needed by infant children are covered, except for 'Making predictions' and 'Using equipment', which are best tackled in the context of a specific scientific enquiry,

Do I need to work through the book in the order of the skills?

You can select the specific **Skill Activities** that you think your class needs to develop. If, for example, you feel that your class lacks confidence in presenting evidence, then turn to that section. You can use the **Skill Activities** in the order that suits you and your class.

How do I know that these Skill Activities will match the level of attainment in my class?

New Star Science has a **Skills Ladder** (see page 5) which describes how children make progress in the different skills as they become older. All the **Skill Activities** are linked to the level of demand suggested for infant children.

How can we make sure that there is progression in skills through the school?

There are similar New Star Science books to help you teach the same skills at lower junior and upper junior levels. They also contain **Skill Activities** matched to the appropriate Year Groups on the **Skills Ladder**.

Can I use this book alongside any scheme of work or other published material?

The **Skill Activities** can be used alongside any scheme of work or other published material, including New Star Science and the QCA scheme of work.

How can I develop children's language skills through this book?

Many of the **Skill Activities** place an emphasis on developing language. However, much can also be done in everyday activities in the infant classroom to help develop the language needed for investigations, especially comparative language. The following is a list of suggestions that might be used.

Activities to encourage comparative language

Activity	What to change	Comparative language
Squeezing dough	Temperature – warm dough, cold dough.	The colder dough is harder to squeeze than the warmer dough.
Riding sit-on toys over different surfaces	Surface – grass, gravel playground, hall floor.	You have to push harder over a rougher surface.
Washing up	Amount of washing-up liquid – big squeeze, little squeeze.	There are more bubbles when you put a lot of washing-up liquid in the water.
Icing a cake	Amount of colouring – 5 drops, 1 drop.	The icing goes darker when you put in more drops of the colouring.
Cooking biscuits	Time cooking – long time, short time.	Biscuits go browner when you leave them in for a longer time.

What is scientific enquiry?

'Scientific enquiry' is a term that encompasses different types of practical work in science. The essential aspect of a scientific enquiry is that children make some decisions about how to go about the enquiry and what to make of the evidence.

There are several ways of carrying out scientific enquiries including:

Fair testing

In these enquiries you change one factor (the independent variable), measure the effect on another factor (the dependent variable), and keep other factors (the control variables) the same to make the test fair. For example, if testing how the temperature of the water affects the time taken for sugar to dissolve, you would change the temperature, measure the time taken to dissolve and keep the container, the volume of water, the number of stirs and the amount and type of sugar the same.

Finding an association

These enquiries usually occur when you are working with animals, including humans, or in the environment. In these contexts, it is often impossible to carry out a fair test because you cannot keep all relevant factors the same. For example, if you wanted to know whether there is a relationship between the height of a person and their pulse rate, you would find it impossible to do a fair test by changing only the height of people and keeping all other factors such as weight, age group and fitness level the same. Instead you see if there is an association between height and pulse rate by measuring these things across a reasonable sample of people.

Classifying

In these enquiries, you arrange a variety of objects or events into sets. It is important that children decide the criteria for sorting into sets, and also pick out other features that the members of the sets have in common. For example if classifying small invertebrates according to the number of legs, they may recognise that all those with six legs have their legs attached to the middle of their three body segments. Or, if classifying materials into those attracted to a magnet and those not attracted to a magnet, they may recognise that only certain metals are attracted.

Exploring

For these enquiries you make careful observations or measurements of objects or events over time. You have to decide what is worth observing or measuring, and how often the observations or measurements should be made. For example, you might study the growth of one bean plant over several weeks, or you might observe how the Moon appears to change shape over several days.

Problem-solving

In these enquiries you find a way to solve a specific problem. You have to design, test and adapt an object or a system. For example, you might find a way to clean dirty water, or to make a flashing light on top of a model Christmas tree.

The majority of science enquiries carried out in primary schools are of the fair-testing type. Likewise, the majority of the **Skill Activities** in this book focus on the skills that children need to carry out a fair test. However, the **Skill Activities** also feature some of the skills needed for other types of scientific enquiry as shown on the table opposite.

Skill Activity	Type of Scientific Enquiry	Skill Activity	Type of Scientific Enquiry
1	Fair testing	16	Fair testing
2	Fair testing	17	Fair testing
3	Various	18	Fair testing
4	Various	19	Fair testing
5	Various	20	Exploring
6	Various	21	Exploring and Fair testing
7	Fair testing	22	Fair testing
8	Fair testing	23	Fair testing
9	Various	24	Classifying
10	Fair testing	25	Fair testing
11	Fair testing	26	Fair testing
12	Fair testing	27	Fair testing
13	Various	28	Finding an Association
14	Various	29	Fair testing
15	Exploring	30	Fair testing

Skills Ladder

New Star Science covers all the skills used in scientific enquiry. However, it is vital that you increase the complexity and demand of these skills as children go through the school. New Star Science is built around the **Skills Ladder** which outlines how the skills of scientific enquiry build from year to year. This framework ensures that your children progress in scientific enquiry.

The **Skills Ladder** is organised under three main headings: Planning; Obtaining and presenting evidence; and Considering evidence and evaluating. The appropriate skills for each year (R to 6) are listed under these headings.

By working through the New Star Science Units, the children will naturally climb the **Skills Ladder**. Within each Unit, several skills areas are covered, although there are some Units where practical work is difficult to carry out and the skills have less emphasis, such as Earth, Sun and Moon. Most New Star Science Units provide a good range of skills work, allowing flexibility, even if all the Units are not used.

All the activities in this book are linked to the level of demand suggested for infant children in the **Skills Ladder**. Most of the **Skill Activities** are pitched at National Curriculum level 1, 2 (levels A, B, C in Scotland). You will find extra guidance about the level of demand in the Teacher's Notes.

New Star Science Skills Ladder

	Planning				
	Asking questions and having ideas	**Deciding an appropriate approach**	**Planning the detail of what to do**	**Predicting what might happen**	**Choosing what equipment to use**
R	Asks questions about objects and events. Tries out things when handling equipment	Tries out different approaches suggested to them.	Sometimes suggests next step in a plan.	Sometimes suggests what might happen in a specific instance in response to teacher's prompt.	Recognises that different equipment is needed for different things.
Year 1	Asks questions using a range of question stems e.g. How? What will happen if? Why? Tests ideas suggested to them.	With support, identifies questions that can be answered by trying it out and those that cannot.	Suggests next step, or steps, in a plan.	Suggests what might happen in a specific instance in response to teacher's prompt.	Begins to choose appropriate equipment from a limited range with support from the teacher.
Year 2	With support, asks questions leading to scientific enquiry.	Sorts questions into those that can be answered by trying it out and those that cannot.	With support, describes the observations or measurements they need to take, spots when a plan will lead to an unfair test and recognises hazards.	With support, sometimes predicts outcomes of enquiries.	Chooses appropriate equipment from a limited range with support from the teacher.
Year 3	Sometimes asks questions leading to scientific enquiry.	Knows there are different ways of answering scientific questions.	In a fair test, identifies what to keep the same. With support plans main steps in other types of enquiry. Recognises most hazards.	Sometimes predicts outcomes to enquiries.	Selects appropriate equipment from a wider range with support from the teacher.
Year 4	Asks questions and offers own ideas for scientific enquiry.	With support knows when to answer a question by using a fair test and when evidence should be collected in other ways.	In a fair test, identifies what to keep the same and with support what to change and what to measure/observe. Plans main steps in other enquiries. Recognises hazards and, with support, plans how to control risks.	Predicts outcomes and sometimes suggests reasons for their prediction.	Selects appropriate equipment and with support, considers the scale and the degree of accuracy required on some measuring equipment.
Year 5	Asks questions and offers own ideas for scientific enquiry and, with support, improves question to clarify scientific purpose.	Knows when to answer a question by using a fair test and when evidence should be collected in other ways, including using secondary sources.	Sets up a fair test knowing what to change/measure/observe and what to keep the same. With support considers whether to take repeat readings. With support, plans the detail in other types of enquiry. Assesses hazards and plans how to control risks.	Predicts outcomes and, where appropriate, suggests reasons for their predictions.	Selects equipment from a wider range, including digital scales, forcemeters and computer sensors. With support, considers the scale and the degree of accuracy required on measuring equipment.
Year 6	Asks questions and offers own ideas for scientific enquiry which have a clear scientific purpose.	Identifies appropriate approach to answer a scientific question.	Sets up a fair test. Plans the detail in other types of enquiry. With support considers whether plans will yield enough evidence for the task. Assesses hazards and plans how to control risks.	Predicts outcomes and, where appropriate sketches a graph to show the expected pattern in results. Justifies their predictions using scientific knowledge when possible.	Selects suitable equipment for a range of tasks. Takes into account the scale and the degree of accuracy required on measuring equipment.

Obtaining and presenting evidence			Considering evidence and evaluating			
Using equipment and carrying out practical work safely	Making observations and taking measurements	Presenting evidence	Drawing conclusions and describing patterns and trends	Comparing results to predictions and making further predictions	Explaining evidence	Evaluating
Follows instructions for using equipment, usually under adult supervision.	Observes simple features.	Uses drawings to present evidence and with support, uses prepared simple tables, and charts.	With support, describes a simple observation made.	Recognises results that are unexpected.	Responds to prompts about cause and effect in simple situations.	With support, recognises some of the difficulties encountered.
Follows instructions for using equipment correctly and safely, sometimes working without adult support.	Makes relevant observations. With support, takes some non-standard measurements.	Uses drawings and labels to present evidence. With support, uses prepared simple tables and charts.	Describes simple observations made and with support, makes a simple comparison.	With support, says whether what happened was expected in a specific instance.	With support, recognises cause and effect in simple situations.	With support, recognises some of the difficulties encountered.
Follows instructions for using equipment correctly and safely, usually working without adult support.	Makes relevant observations. Takes non-standard measurements. Begins to use basic equipment for measuring quantities such as length or mass, in standard units.	Uses drawings and labels to present evidence. Uses prepared tables and block graphs.	Describes what happened, making comparisons where appropriate. With support, orders results where appropriate.	Says whether what happened was expected. With support, makes further predictions from results in simple contexts.	Recognises cause and effect in most simple situations.	Recognises some of the difficulties encountered. With support, suggests how these might be avoided.
Uses basic equipment correctly and safely. Usually refers to adult when equipment fails.	Makes relevant observations. Uses standard measuring equipment for quantities such as temperature and volume.	Sometimes creates own tables and bar charts.	With support, makes a general statement about some simple patterns in results.	With support, makes further predictions from results in simple contexts.	With support, provides explanations for simple patterns in results.	Recognises the difficulties encountered. With support suggests how the enquiry might be improved.
Uses basic equipment correctly and safely. Begins to deal with equipment failures.	Makes a series of observations. Uses standard measuring equipment for measuring most quantities.	Creates own tables and bar charts. Uses a line chart with support.	Makes a general statement about simple patterns in results.	Makes further predictions from results in simple contexts.	Provides explanations for simple patterns in results.	Suggests how the enquiry might be improved. With support, recognises some of the limitations of their evidence.
Uses a wide range of equipment correctly and safely. Deals with most equipment failures independently.	Makes a series of relevant observations. With support, takes accurate readings on measuring equipment, repeating them where necessary.	Begins to select appropriate way to present evidence. Creates own bar charts and tables, including those for repeat readings. Creates a line graph with support.	With support describes relationships identified, linking both factors and describing whole relationship in comparative terms.	With support, makes further predictions from results and uses these to test out the suggested pattern in the relationship studied.	Sometimes relates patterns in results to scientific knowledge where appropriate.	Identifies how much to trust results. Suggests reasons why similar enquiries yield different results. With support considers the spread of repeated measurements. With support, recognises some of the limitations of their evidence.
Uses a wide range of equipment correctly and safely. Deals with equipment failures independently.	Makes a series of relevant observations. Takes accurate readings on measuring equipment, repeating them where necessary.	Selects suitable way to present evidence. Where appropriate, draws up line graph independently, except where scales involve very large or very small numbers.	Describes relationships identified, linking both factors and describing whole relationship in comparative terms.	Makes further predictions from results and uses these to test out the suggested pattern in the relationship studied.	Relates patterns in results to scientific knowledge where appropriate.	Identifies how much to trust results and justifies decision. Suggests reasons why similar enquiries yield different results. Considers the spread of repeated measurements. Recognises some of the limitations of their evidence

Curriculum Links

New Star Science Skills Ladder		England National Curriculum Key Stage 1	Wales National Curriculum Key Stage 1	Northern Ireland Curriculum Key Stage 1	Scotland 5-14 National Guidelines
Planning	Asking questions and having ideas	Sc1 2a, b	The Nature of Science 1, 2, 3 Investigative Skills 1, 2	Planning (b)	Preparing for the task (levels A, B)
	Deciding an appropriate approach	Sc1 2a, b	Investigative Skills 3	Planning (d, e)	Preparing for tasks (levels A, B)
	Planning the detail of what to do	Sc1 2c, d	Investigative Skills 3	Planning (e, f)	Preparing for tasks (levels A, B, C)
	Predicting what might happen	Sc1 2c, d	Investigative Skills 2	Planning (b)	Preparing for tasks (levels A, B)
	Choosing what equipment to use	Sc1 2c, d	Investigative Skills 3	Planning (e)	Preparing for tasks (levels A, B)
Obtaining and presenting evidence	Using equipment and carrying out practical work safely	Sc1 2e	Investigative Skills 5, 7	Carrying out and making (a, b, g)	Carrying out tasks (levels A, B)
	Making observations and taking measurements	Sc1 2f	Investigative Skills 6, 8	Carrying out and making (d, f)	Carrying out tasks (levels A, B)
	Presenting evidence	Sc1 2g	Communication in Science – all Investigative Skills 9	Carrying out and making (c, h)	Carrying out tasks (levels A, B)
Considering evidence and evaluating	Drawing conclusions and describing patterns and trends	Sc1 2h	Investigative Skills 10, 11	Interpreting and Evaluating (b, e, g)	Reviewing and reporting on tasks (levels A, B)
	Comparing results to predictions and making further predictions	Sc1 2i	Investigative Skills 10, 11	Interpreting and Evaluating (b, c, e)	Reviewing and reporting on tasks (levels A, B)
	Explaining evidence	Sc1 2i	Investigative Skills 12	Interpreting and Evaluating (c, g)	Reviewing and reporting on tasks (levels A, B)
	Evaluating	Sc1 2j	Investigative Skills 13	Interpreting and Evaluating (f, h)	Reviewing and reporting on tasks (levels A, B)

Asking questions and having ideas

Encouraging children's ideas and questions is central to science, but not all children have either the ability or confidence to offer them. Try to offer children lots of opportunities to share ideas, to offer suggestions and to learn how to phrase questions.
Sometimes, by putting things into a story context or by rephrasing a question, we can encourage children to become more involved.

Skill Activity 1

Teaching strategy: *Worst case scenarios*

Purpose

To encourage children to put forward their own ideas for investigating.

Skill Activity 2

Teaching strategy: *Looking at each part in turn*

Purpose

To encourage children to generate questions by looking at the different parts or aspects of whatever they are investigating.

Skill Activity 3

Teaching strategy: *Encouraging questions through display*

Purpose

To value children's questions and ideas.

Skill Activity 4

Pupil activity: *My questions*

Purpose

To encourage children to ask questions.

What to do

Ask the children to work together to think of questions about whatever they are studying. Talk about the words and phrases we use to start questions such as 'where', 'what', 'why', 'which', 'when', 'what will happen if...', 'how'. Tell them that you are particularly looking for questions that need a test or scientific investigation to find the answer. Say that the question starters 'which'; 'how'; 'what will happen if...' are often used for questions that can be answered by testing.

Ask them to suggest their ideas for questions to the person next to them and to complete the worksheet. If they have any other questions they want to include, ask them to write the question on the back of the worksheet. Possible questions include:

- Which paper is strongest?

- Which car goes furthest?

- How deep should we plant our seeds?

- How can I stop my ice cube from melting so quickly?

- How can I make the bulb light?

- What will happen if I put the ramp higher?

- What will happen if I bang the drum harder?

Asking questions and having ideas

Skill Activity 1 *Teaching strategy*

Worst case scenarios – *to encourage children to put forward their own ideas for investigating*

Children often find it easier to suggest ideas for testing if you set up 'worst case scenarios'.

For example: a car that rolls a very short distance, a ball that hardly bounces, some sugar that takes ages to dissolve, or an ice cube th melts very quickly. Once you have shown the children a worst case scenario, you can ask them for their ideas for making; the car go further, the ball bounce higher, the sugar dissolve faster or the ice cubes melt more quickly.

Example

Car on the ramp

In this investigation, the children measure the distance the car travels. The factors that might affect this are: the height of the ramp, the starting point on the ramp and the surface the car runs onto, assuming the same car is used. Set up the equipment like this:

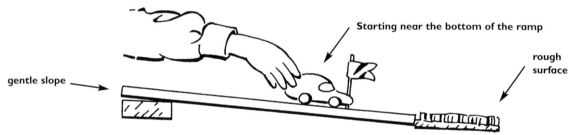

Starting near the bottom of the ramp

rough surface

gentle slope

Let the car go and explain to the children how disappointed you are that it only went a short distance. Ask the children if they can suggest things that would make it go further. If you want a record of their ideas, ask them to draw pictures of their suggestions.

Example

Bouncing balls

In this investigation, children measure or observe how high the ball bounces. The factors that might affect this are: the height of drop, the type of ball and the type of surface the ball is dropped onto. Set up the investigation as suggested by the picture.

Drop the ball and point out that the ball hardly bounces. Ask the children for their ideas for getting a higher bounce.

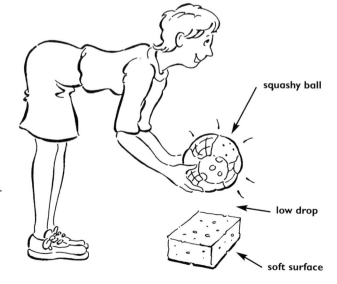

squashy ball

low drop

soft surface

Asking questions and having ideas

Skill Activity 2 *Teaching strategy*

Looking at each part in turn – *to encourage children to generate questions by looking at the different parts or aspects of whatever they are investigating.*

If you break down whatever you are investigating into small parts, children often find it easier to ask questions that are suitable for investigating.

> ### Example
>
> When children investigate plant growth there are many things that might affect how well the plant grows. If you have already planted seeds with the children, they should be able to tell you the steps to take to plant the seeds. At each step in the process, challenge the children to think how it could be altered (see pictures). Putting other equipment on display can help to stimulate questions.
>
>
>
> Ask the children to think about each part in turn. Then get them to suggest questions which they could investigate. You may find it helps to give them the start of the question, e.g. 'What will happen if ..?'

Asking questions and having ideas

Skill Activity 3 *Teaching strategy*

Encouraging questions through display

Children love seeing their questions displayed in different ways or being asked to post them. Promoting their questions like this shows that we value their ideas and questions as much as we value their answers.

Example

Make a question mobile

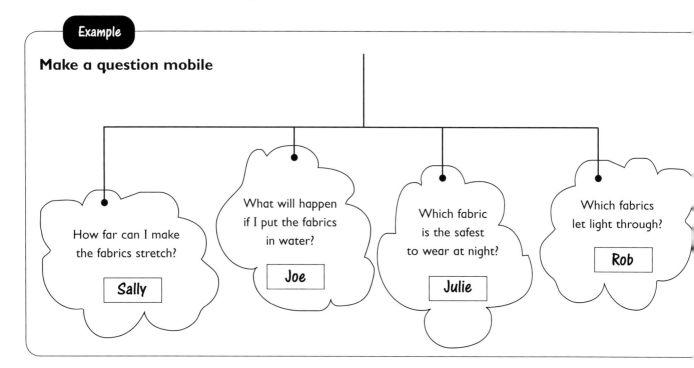

How far can I make the fabrics stretch?

Sally

What will happen if I put the fabrics in water?

Joe

Which fabric is the safest to wear at night?

Julie

Which fabrics let light through?

Rob

Example

Make a question tree

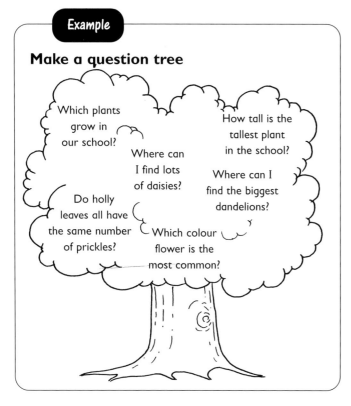

Which plants grow in our school?

How tall is the tallest plant in the school?

Where can I find lots of daisies?

Where can I find the biggest dandelions?

Do holly leaves all have the same number of prickles?

Which colour flower is the most common?

Example

Post a question

POST

POST

Let's see what's in our questions postbox.

ame ....

ly questions

hink of some questions to ask.
omplete the sentences.

ly question is about _____

_____

Vhich _____

_____

ow _____

_____

Vhat will happen if _____

_____

_____

Deciding on an approach

There are several ways of getting evidence through scientific enquiry. These include fair testing, finding an association, classifying, exploring and problem-solving. Before tackling a scientific question, we have to decide on a suitable approach. Infant children do not need to be able to sort all their scientific enquiries into one of these categories. They only need to begin to become aware that there are different ways of finding answers to questions. The first **Skill Activity** in this section asks them to sort questions into those that can be answered by using books and those that can be answered by 'doing' something. The second **Skill Activity** also asks them to consider which questions can be answered using a book, but sub-divides the doing section into looking and testing.

Skill Activity 5

Teaching strategy: *How shall we find out?*

Purpose

To know that questions can be answered using books
or by doing something.

Skill Activity 6

Pupil activity: *What would you do?*

Purpose

To decide how to find answers.

What to do

Ask the children to look at the questions about balls. Discuss the various ways of finding out answers to questions and point out the symbols used to represent them. Get them to sort the questions, working in pairs, followed by a class discussion about their responses. See if they can add some more questions to the list.

Deciding on an approach

Skill Activity 5 *Teaching strategy*

How shall we find out?

This activity is a first step in helping children to decide on an appropriate approach. It asks them to decide how they might answer a question. They have a choice of either using a book or doing something.

Provide each child with a wipe-clean board or a piece of card with the following on each side.

book

do

Ask them to hold up the sign that shows how they would find the answer to a question.

Example

Name ....

What would you do?

look

book

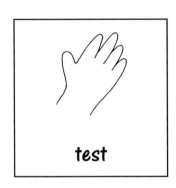

test

How would you find out the answer to these questions about balls? Write or draw in the boxes.

Which ball bounces highest?

How is a football made?

What are the balls made from?

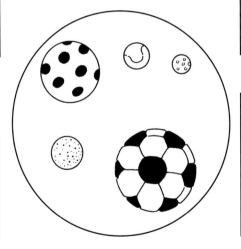

Which ball is biggest?

Which ball squashes the most?

Which ball rolls furthest?

Planning what to do

Young children can find it hard to think ahead to plan an activity. Rather than asking them to plan out a whole enquiry, the first three activities focus on asking them about the next step in a plan, or on sequencing a series of steps. Two of the **Skill Activities** introduce young children to the idea of fair testing. When we carry out an investigation, we must only change one factor at a time and keep all other factors the same. If we change more than one factor, we will not be able to tell what is causing the effect. For example, if we drop parachutes of different sizes and materials, and find out that some fall more slowly than others, we will be unable to say whether it is the size or the material (or both) that is affecting the rate of descent. When we ask children to tell us how they made a test fair, we want them to tell us how they kept some factors the same. However, quite reasonably, young children often assume that we are asking how we can make it fair to them, e.g. by giving every member of the group a turn at doing something. These two activities aim to help children understand what 'being fair' means in a scientific sense. In the final activity, children identify possible hazards in science activities.

Skill Activity 7

Teaching strategy: *What should we do next?*

Purpose

To consider the next step when planning a scientific enquiry.

Skill Activity 8

Teaching strategy: *Getting muddled up*

Purpose

To help children clarify their plans.

Skill Activity 9

Pupil activity: *My plan*

Purpose

To help children think ahead.

What to do

This sheet assumes that you will have already decided on the question to investigate. It is a simple worksheet, which is designed for children to draw pictures about what they will do and what they think will happen. Tell the children that they do not have to put a picture (or words) in every box and that they can draw more pictures if they run out of room. Make sure that you look at their plans and talk to them about their ideas, before they tackle the practical work.

Skill Activity 10

Teaching strategy: *Making it a fair competition*

Purpose

To help children understand fair testing by turning the investigation into a competition.

Skill Activity 11

Teaching strategy: *Deliberately making it unfair*

Purpose

To enable children to spot when a test is unfair.

Skill Activity 12

Pupil activity: *Fair testing*

Purpose

To distinguish between a fair and an unfair test.

What to do

Make sure that the children understand what the investigation is about before you ask them to complete the worksheet. As it is a different material that is being tested (orange squash and water) all other factors should be kept the same. The children should spot that it is unfair on two counts. Firstly, the ice cubes are of different sizes when they should be the same, and secondly they are left in places of different temperatures (one is above the radiator) when this should also be the same.

Skill Activity 13

Pupil activity: *Stop!*

Purpose

To identify possible risks in practical work.

What to do

Infant children should be able to identify risks to themselves and others when doing practical work. Whilst teachers take responsibility for children's safety, we still want them to be aware of possible dangers. The activity on this worksheet asks them to identify some risks.

Planning what to do

Skill Activity 7 *Teaching strategy*

What should we do next?

We can encourage children to think ahead and plan by asking what the next step would be.

Using *talk partners* is a good way of involving more children in planning. A talk partner is a friend or someone they are sitting next to that they are happy to talk to. Children often need to practise their language skills, and using talk partners gives them all the chance to speak the words to someone else. It also builds confidence.

Planning what to do

Skill Activity 8 *Teaching strategy*

Getting muddled up

Once the children know what question they are trying to answer in the investigation, ask them to tell you how to go about it. As they give you an instruction, carry out what they say, even though the instructions may be wrong, out of sequence or unclear. The children will soon put you right and, in doing so, clarify their own plans. Alternatively, draw cartoon pictures showing children what they will do in their investigation.

Put the pictures in the wrong sequence. Ask them to cut out and then stick the pictures in the right order.

Example

These plans are in a muddle. Cut out the pictures and put them in the right order.

Which tights stretch the most?

Count the number of hand spans on the paper strip.

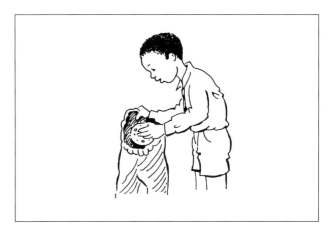

Put an orange down one leg of the tights.

Cut off a strip of paper that goes from toe to toe.

Which tights?	How much they stretched
Grey	6 hand spans
Brown	
Black	

Write down the number of hand spans on your table.

Name ....

My plan

First I will:	**Next I will:**
Then I will:	**After that I will:**

What I think will happen:

Planning what to do

Skill Activity 10 *Teaching strategy*

Making it a fair competition

When young children are asked to make a test fair, they sometimes have difficulty in knowing what is wanted. For many children, fairness involves every child in the group having a go at doing something, rather than the scientific meaning of keeping everything the same, other than the one factor that is being changed.

In order to help children understand what is meant by making it fair, you can turn the investigation into a competition and personalise the competitors. In this way, the children talk about how to make the test fair for the competitors and, in doing so, get a better understanding of fair testing.

Example

1 Dissolving jelly in water of different temperatures.

Hussein Hot Water, Mary Medium Water and Carl Cool Water are having a competition. They want to see who can be the quickest at making the jelly go into the water. How can we make it fair for the three competitors, Hussein, Mary and Carl?

How hot the water is	How quickly the Jelly goes into the water
Hussein Hot Water	
Mary Medium Water	
Carl Cool Water	

Example

2 Stopping light – shining a torch through different papers.

There is a competition between different papers to see which one blocks out more light. We must make it fair for the competitors Tammy Tissue Paper, Shareen Sugar Paper and Graham Greaseproof Paper.

Which paper	How much light is blocked
Tammy Tissue Paper	
Shareen Sugar Paper	
Graham Greaseproof Paper	

Planning what to do

Skill Activity 11 *Teaching strategy*

Deliberately making it unfair

One way to help children to understand the idea of making a test fair, is to do a demonstration where you deliberately make things unfair. Ask the children to put up their hands or call out 'That's not fair!' whenever they spot you going wrong (the latter option of calling out can become a little like the 'He's behind you' routine at a pantomime – noisy, but good fun). When they have identified something unfair, ask them to explain why it's not fair. Using talk partners for this, helps to involve all the children.

Example

Which dissolves first, soft brown sugar or granulated white sugar?

ame ....

air testing

ome children had an orange squash ice block

nd a water ice block.

hey wanted to find out which melts faster.

he picture shows what they did.

orange squash ice block ▲   water ice block ▲

their test fair? Put a   ✓   Yes ☐   No ☐

What would you do? Draw or write.

Name ....

Stop!

Look at these pictures. What would you say to these children?

I'll drop my parachute from the table.

Stop! Don't _____

_____

_____

_____

_____

Stop! Don't _____

_____

_____

_____

_____

Yum! These look tasty!

Look at the bright Sun!

Stop! Don't _____

_____

_____

_____

_____

Choosing equipment

Choosing the right equipment is an important aspect of science. If you want children to start choosing the equipment they should use, you need to offer them limited choices with large differences; for example, you could ask them to say whether they should use large steps, or interlinking cubes to measure a plant leaf.

You will also need to teach them how to use measuring equipment. Even if you use non-standard equipment such as lolly sticks to measure length, you will need to teach them to put the first stick at the start, to keep the sticks straight, to avoid over-lapping or large gaps and how to deal with the inevitable 'bit left over'. Many of the measuring skills they need will be similar to those used in mathematics, but it is often worth quickly reminding them before they tackle an investigation.

The following **Skills Activities** concentrate on *choosing* the equipment. Teaching young children how to use equipment is most easily done first-hand with the class measuring equipment.

Skill Activity 14

Teaching strategy: *Silly ideas*

Purpose

To choose suitable equipment from a limited range.

What to do

This activity offers silly ways of measuring. Ask the children if they can think of better ways of measuring. What would they use, why would they use that?

Skill Activity 15

Pupil activity: *Which one?*

Purpose

To choose suitable equipment for measuring length.

What to do

This activity asks children to decide what they should use to measure the distance someone can jump. In this instance, the choice is from both non-standard measures (interlinking cubes, straws and string) and standard measures (tape measure, ruler). The choice here largely depends on ease of use, as the interlinking cubes, straws and small ruler would all involve practical difficulties (e.g. take too long, difficult to keep straight, need to move up repeatedly). Cutting the string would give a direct measurement, but you could not tell others how far you jumped without having the string with you at all times. The tape measure avoids all these difficulties. However, children may quite reasonably select one of the other methods. Let them use the other equipment and discuss afterwards how they got on with their equipment.

The activity also asks children to use their choice of equipment to measure each other's jump. They could then draw or write what they did and thus enable you to check they are measuring correctly.

Choosing equipment

Skill Activity 14 *Teaching strategy*

Silly ideas

One way of helping children to choose the right equipment is to make silly suggestions.
The more extreme something is, the more sensible the alternative seems to the child.

Example

> I think I will measure how long this leaf is in foot lengths. I will walk down the leaf and see how many of my feet it is.
>
> Is that a good idea? What would you use to measure it?

Example

> I'm going to use a ruler to find out how much water is in these containers.
>
> Is that a good idea? What would you use?

ame ....

Which one?

Which one would you use to measure how far someone can jump?

ut a ☐✓

 ☐

cubes

 ☐

straws

 ☐

string

 ☐

small ruler

 ☐

tape measure

Write and draw to show how you would use it.

Now, work in pairs to measure your jumps. Take turns.
Are you measuring the right way?

Presenting evidence

If you introduce work on tables to young children, you must first check that they share your meaning of the word 'table'. To most children it is something with four legs that they sit at to do their work or eat their dinner. They need to know that it has another meaning in science, or they are likely to be mystified by any request to 'put your results on a table'! Tables are great organisers. If you help children to prepare a table as part of their plan, they are much more likely to carry out their investigations systematically. Another benefit of tables is that they convey a lot of information with very little writing, so children can take a number of planning decisions without having to write copious amounts of text. These **Skill Activities** will help children to learn why we use tables, and to start to know how to set up a simple 2-column table.

This section also helps children learn how to construct a pictograph, and then a block graph, from information given on a table. Some of the investigations that you undertake may not lead to block graphs, particularly those undertaken with very young children where no measurements are taken and children just make observations. However, when your investigation does lead to a block graph, make the most of the opportunity, either by using a class block graph or by asking higher attaining children to make their own.

Skill Activity 16

Teaching strategy: *Working backwards from a table to the investigation*

Purpose

To become familiar with the structure of a table and the information recorded on it.

Skill Activity 17

Teaching strategy: *Why do we use tables?*

Purpose

To know that it is easier to get information from a table than from text.

Skill Activity 18

Pupil activity: *Find what's wrong*

Purpose

To know how to use a 2-column table.

What to do

Make sure that the children understand what is going on in the investigation on the worksheet and help them to study the pictures. Ask the children to look at the table and tell them that some mistakes have been made. It is their job to spot them and then write the table correctly.

The three things they should spot are:

1 The plant in sand grew 7 blocks high not 8 blocks.

2 The plant in peat grew 9 blocks high not 10 blocks.

3 The word gravel should replace the number 6 in the first column

Ask them to fill in the blank table with the correct words and values.

Skill Activity 19

Pupil activity: *Using a table*

Purpose

To know how to construct a 2-column table.

What to do

Use this **Skill Activity** with children who feel confident about filling in information on a table. Make sure they understand what is happening in the pictures on the worksheet and then tell them this is a chance to show that they know how to use a table. Ask them to complete the table from the information in the pictures.

Skill Activity 20

Teaching strategy: *Make a class pictograph*

Purpose

To show information on a pictograph.

Skill Activity 21

Teaching strategy: *From direct measurement to a block graph*

Purpose

To show how a block graph represents measurements.

Skill Activity 22

Teaching strategy: *Moving information from a table to a block graph*

Purpose

To know how to transfer information from a table to a block graph.

Skill Activity 23

Teaching strategy: *Spot the mistakes*

Purpose

To know how to draw up a block graph from a table.

What to do

Make sure the children know what the investigation on the worksheet is about. Ask them to spot the mistakes on the block graph.

They should notice:

1 The second label on the horizontal axis should say 'wood' not sand paper'.

2 The horizontal axis should be labelled 'Material'.

3 The column for the 'sand' reads 3 cm rather than 2 cm.

4 The column for the 'stones' reads 2 cm rather than 1 cm.

Presenting evidence

Skill Activity 16 *Teaching strategy*

Working backwards from the table to the investigation

We want children to know how to set up tables for themselves. However, young children are often unclear about the sort of information that we put in tables. One way to help them is to show them a completed table and ask them to say what they think the investigation was about; in other words to work back from the table to the investigation. Try to bring out the importance of the headings and show that the things that are being tested (or the competitors, see Skill Activity 10).

Example

Talk to the children about the structure of the table, pointing out that it has two columns, each with a heading at the top. Read the words in the table with the children. Ask questions such as:

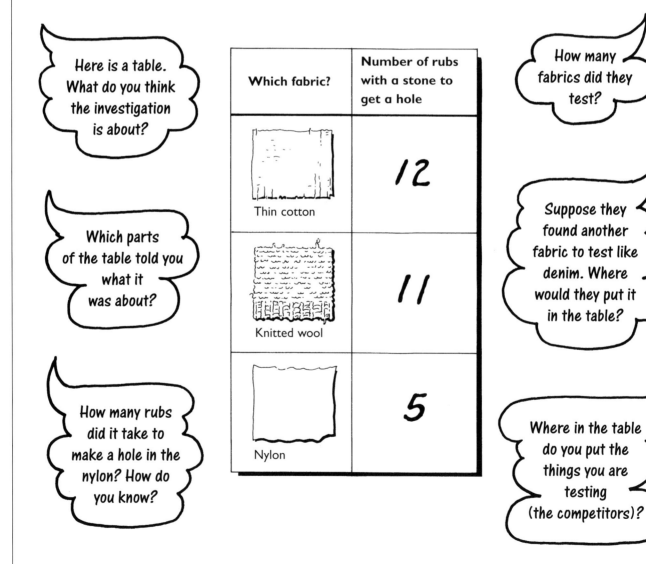

Here is a table. What do you think the investigation is about?

Which parts of the table told you what it was about?

How many rubs did it take to make a hole in the nylon? How do you know?

Which fabric?	Number of rubs with a stone to get a hole
Thin cotton	12
Knitted wool	11
Nylon	5

How many fabrics did they test?

Suppose they found another fabric to test like denim. Where would they put it in the table?

Where in the table do you put the things you are testing (the competitors)?

Presenting evidence

Skill Activity 17 *Teaching strategy*

Why do we use tables?

One of the reasons that we use tables is because it is easier to get information from tables than from written prose. We can help children to recognize this by using both text and tables to access the same information and discussing which they found the simplest to use.

Draw up large versions of the same information written in text and recorded in a table, such as that shown below.

Example

We had three cars. We let the red one go first. It went four straws. Next we tried the blue car. It went a long way. It went nine straws. Last of all we let the green car go. It went seven straws.

Car	How far it went
Red car	4 straws
Blue car	9 straws
Green car	7 straws

Hold up both versions in front of the children and quickly ask a question such as 'How far did the blue car go?' or 'Which car went 7 straws?'. Ask the children to point to the place where they found the answer. Ask them why they used the table rather than the text to find the answer. They should notice that it is much easier to get information from a table.

Name ....

Find what's wrong

Some children grew bean plants. They grew them in sand, soil and gravel. They used blocks to measure them. This is what happened.

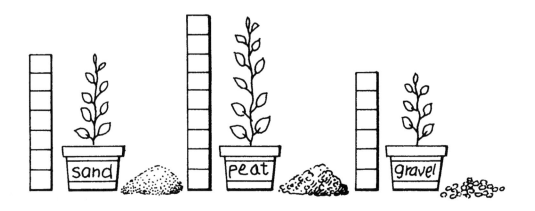

They drew a table. There were 3 mistakes in their table. Put a ring around the mistakes.

Which soil?	How many blocks high?
sand	8
peat	10
6	6

Fill in the empty boxes on this table.

Which soil?	How many blocks high?

ame ....

Using a table

Some children did a test with socks.

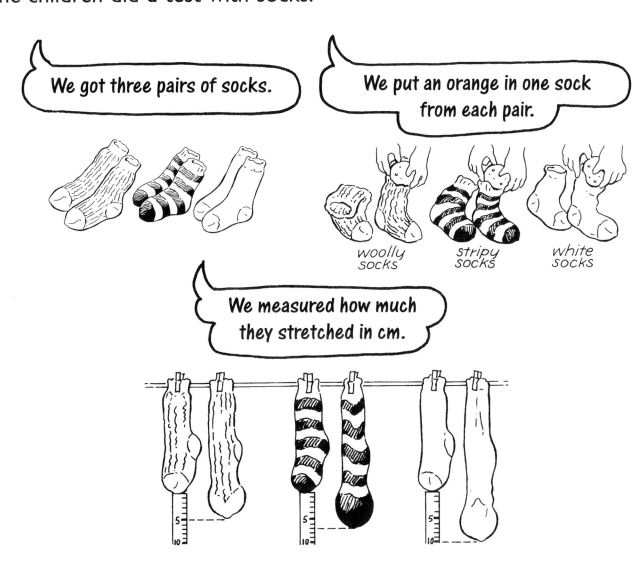

We got three pairs of socks.

We put an orange in one sock
from each pair.

woolly
socks

stripy
socks

white
socks

We measured how much
they stretched in cm.

What should their table look
like? Fill in the blanks.

Which socks?	How much they stretched

Presenting evidence

Skill Activity 20 *Teaching strategy*

Make a class pictograph

When you want children to start representing information on charts, it is a good idea to start with a class pictograph.
You can invite children to come out and stick things on the pictograph. Ask questions as the pictograph gradually emerges.

If you are using irregular shaped objects like leaves to stick on, it is a good idea to prepare boxes on the chart.
In this way 5 small leaves will, make a taller column than 3 large leaves.

Example

Which plants have we found on our field?

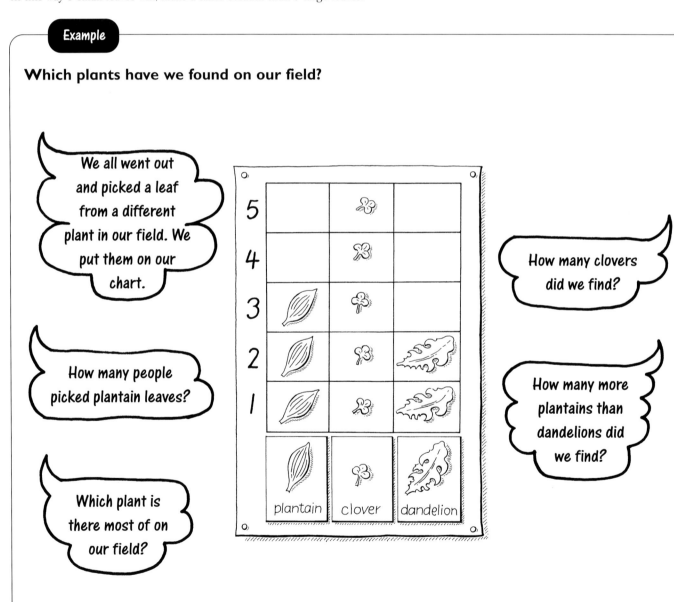

We all went out and picked a leaf from a different plant in our field. We put them on our chart.

How many people picked plantain leaves?

Which plant is there most of on our field?

How many clovers did we find?

How many more plantains than dandelions did we find?

Presenting evidence

Skill Activity 21 *Teaching strategy*

From direct measurement to a block graph

If you are measuring length, it is possible to make a class block graph without using any measuring equipment. Simply cut a strip of squared paper to match the required length and paste this onto your prepared class block graph. Alternatively, build up towers of interlinking cubes, to match the required length or height.

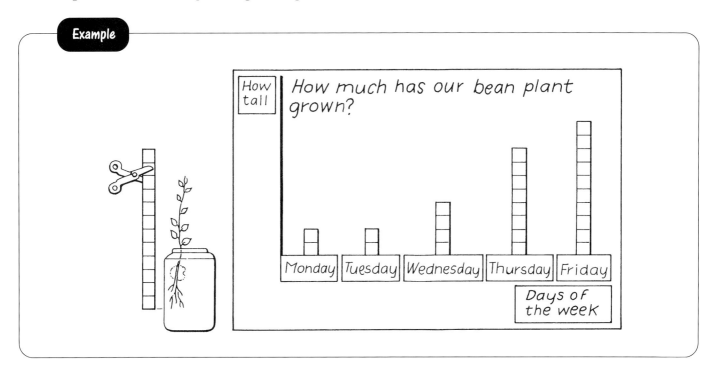

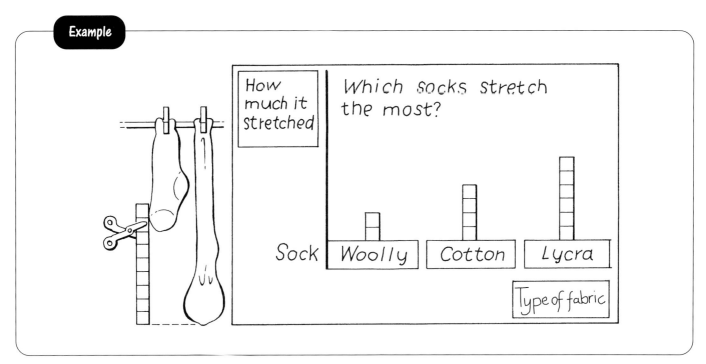

Presenting evidence

Skill Activity 22 *Teaching strategy*

Moving information from a table to a block graph

We often ask children to make a block graph from information in a table. It is well worth spending time with the class, or group, showing children how to do this. Make up a large table and put all the information onto sticky labels or pieces of paper stuck on with Blu-tack. Invite children in turn to move the stickers from the table to the class block graph, or to swap a sticker for a column which can also be stuck on the graph.

ame ....

pot the mistakes

ere is a table some children drew. hey used this table to draw a ock graph.

Material	How far the car went
sand paper	4 cm
wood	10 cm
sand	2 cm
stones	1 cm

here are some mistakes on their block graph. ow many can you spot? ut a ring around them.

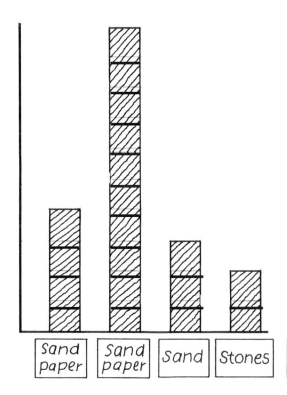

Drawing conclusions and describing patterns in results

Young children often find it difficult to draw a good conclusion. When we ask children to draw a conclusion, we want them to sum up what their evidence tells them in a short clear statement. The first requirement is that children's statements about their results must match the evidence. Encourage the children to say as much as possible about the results in their tables and block graph. It can help them to see patterns and trends if the results are put in order. We also want to encourage children to make statements about the pattern in all their results, and not just about the one that was 'best'.

Skill Activity 24

Teaching strategy: *Puppet talk*

Purpose

To match conclusions drawn to the evidence shown in a table.

Skill Activity 25

Teaching strategy: *Awarding prizes*

Purpose

To order results on a table.

Skill Activity 26

Teaching strategy: *Putting things in order*

Purpose

To order results on a block graph.

Skill Activity 27

Pupil activity: *Can I say that?*

Purpose

To compare statements against the evidence shown in a block graph.

What to do

Before the children can decide whether or not the statements match the information on the block graph on the worksheet, you need to be sure that they have read the statements carefully. They should then check the statements against the block graph. Encourage them to carry out this type of check on any investigation that they do.

Skill Activity 28

Pupil activity: *Is that right?*

Purpose

To compare statements with the evidence shown in two block graphs.

What to do

This activity is similar to the previous one except that it requires the children to look at information presented on two block graphs, rather than one. Ask the children to look carefully at all the information on the worksheet before turning to the sentences and checking them against the evidence. If working with a higher attaining group, see if they can work towards a statement that sums up how the length of hand spans is associated with the length of middle fingers, e.g. on the whole children with longer hand spans have longer fingers. When carrying out other scientific enquiries, make up sentences like these and ask the children to evaluate them before they write their own conclusion. Encourage them to carry out this type of check on any investigation that they do.

Drawing conclusions and describing patterns in results

Skill Activity 24 *Teaching strategy*

Puppet talk

Children often respond well to a glove puppet, particularly if the puppet gets things wrong and the children have to put him/her right. Make the puppet draw some incorrect and correct conclusions from the evidence the children have collected. The children have to correct the puppet's mistakes.

Using the table below, make the puppet give statements such as those in the speech bubbles. Ask the children to check the puppet's comments to make sure he/she is correct.

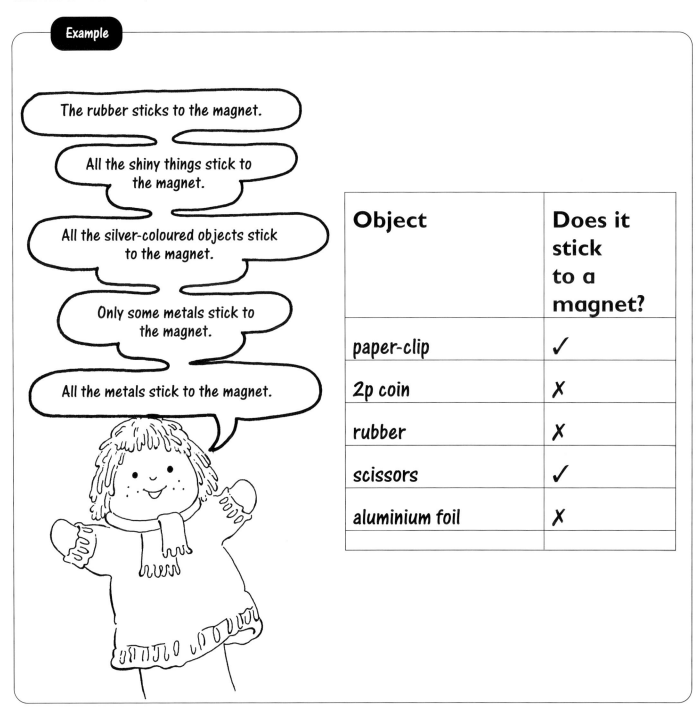

Example

The rubber sticks to the magnet.

All the shiny things stick to the magnet.

All the silver-coloured objects stick to the magnet.

Only some metals stick to the magnet.

All the metals stick to the magnet.

Object	Does it stick to a magnet?
paper-clip	✓
2p coin	✗
rubber	✗
scissors	✓
aluminium foil	✗

Drawing conclusions and describing patterns in results

Skill Activity 25 *Teaching strategy*

Awarding prizes

When beginning investigations with young children, we often put results in a table and use words, rather than numbers, in the second column. We can still encourage children to look more closely at their results by asking them to say which came first, second, third etc. To make things more interesting, award prizes (e.g. stickers, small paper rosettes) to the things that the children tested. This approach works well when tied in with the competitors approach, see Skill Activity 10, page 21.

Draw up the tables onto poster-sized paper to use with the class or a group. Ask the children to help you hand out 'the awards'.

Example

Type of paper	How much light came through?
tissue paper	some (3rd)
kitchen paper	little bit (2nd)
card	none (1st)
clear plastic	lots (4th)

Fabric	How much it stretched?
cotton	(3rd best Stretcher)
wool	(2nd best Stretcher)
elastic	(champion Stretcher)

Drawing conclusions and describing patterns in results

Skill Activity 26 *Teaching strategy*

Putting things in order

One way of encouraging children to look in more detail at their block graphs is to ask them to order their results from least to most; rather than simply asking them to identify the 'best' or 'worst'. Work with the children to make a poster-size block graph of their results. Draw the columns and the labels on the horizontal axis on separate pieces of paper. Use Blu-tack to stick them in random order on the block graph. In this way, you will be able to change the position of the columns. By ordering the columns on the block graph, we can sometimes help children to spot patterns.

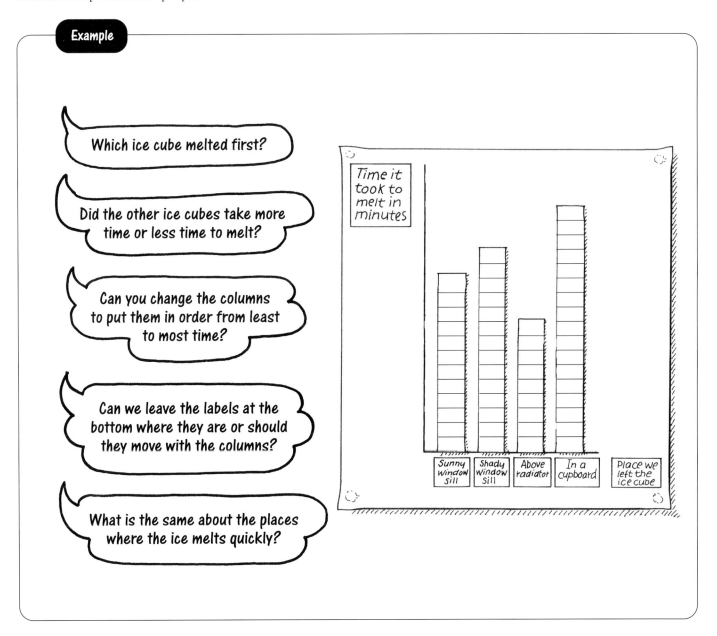

Drawing
conclusions
and describing
patterns in
results

**Skill
Activity 27**

Name ....

Can I say that?

Some children chose 5 toy cars from the
toy basket. They let them go down a slope.
They measured how far they went.
Here is their block graph.

How far
they went
in m

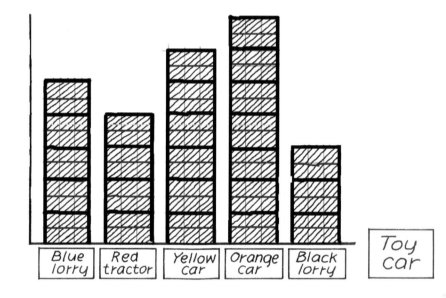

| Blue lorry | Red tractor | Yellow car | Orange car | Black lorry |

Toy
car

Look at the block graph.
Tick one box for each of
these sentences.

The orange car went furthest.

Yes ☐ No ☐

All the toy cars tested went
more than 6 m.

Yes ☐ No ☐

The two lorries went further
than the red tractor.

Yes ☐ No ☐

None of the cars tested went
more than 14 m.

Yes ☐ No ☐

ame ....

that right?

ome children measured their hand spans nd the length of their middle finger centimetres. These are the block graphs f their results.

Hand spans

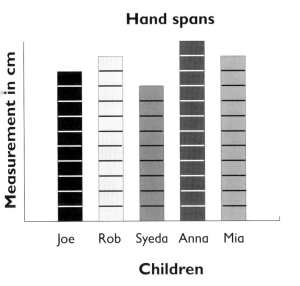

Joe Rob Syeda Anna Mia

Children

Middle fingers

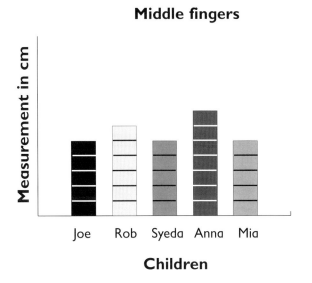

Joe Rob Syeda Anna Mia

Children

ut a ✔ in the correct boxes.

ll the children's hand spans are longer than their middle fingers. ☐

ob's middle finger is 4 cm shorter than his hand span. ☐

our children have the same length middle finger. ☐

he person with the longest hand span has the longest middle finger. ☐

ll the children's middle fingers are between 5 cm and 7 cm long. ☐

Comparing results with predictions and making further prediction

If children have made an initial prediction about the general outcome of a scientific enquiry, we should encourage them to check it against the evidence. This can only be done by working from the children's own statements, so no **Skill Activities** are given. We can also ask them, once they have collected some evidence, to make predictions about things that they have not tested. For example, we could ask them things such as 'Now we know that this car went 10 hand spans when the ramp was on one book, and 18 hand spans when the ramp was on 3 books, how far do you think it will go when the ramp is on two books?'

Young children will find it very difficult to do this task out of context so just one Teaching strategy is offered, which you can apply to many other investigations.

Skill Activity 29

Teaching strategy: *Keeping one behind your back*

Purpose

To make predictions based on evidence collected.

Comparing results with predictions and making further predictions

Skill Activity 29 *Teaching strategy*

Keeping one behind your back

When children have recorded their results and described them, we can help them to use their evidence to make predictions. If you always make sure you have another thing to test 'behind your back', you can put it before the children once the main part of the investigation is over.

Say 'We know about those – but what do you think will happen to this, if we test it the same way?' Always ask the children to justify their prediction.

The first example is much less demanding than the second. It is an easier context, there is less information to consider and the answer will be in words not numbers.

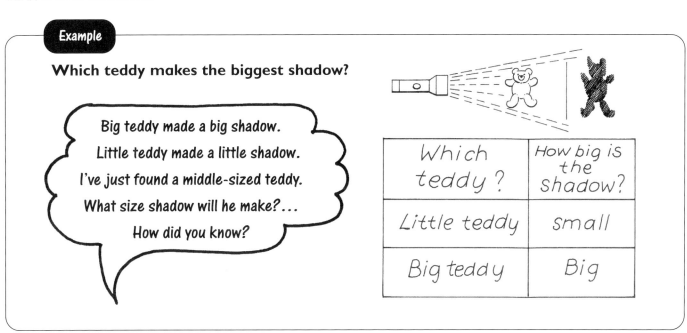

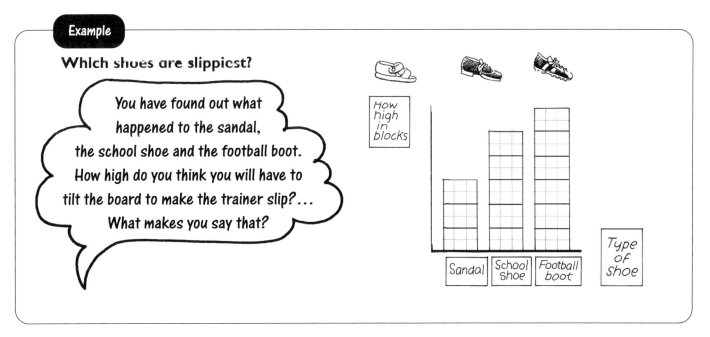

Explaining evidence

Explaining is a difficult skill. It is always worth asking children what they think is causing something to happen, but sometimes the explanations may be beyond their scientific knowledge. Also, whilst we can teach children that most explanations start with the word 'because' it is much harder to teach them the sort of words to put after the 'because'. The **Skill Activity** suggested here asks children to start thinking about what makes a good explanation by getting them to evaluate other children's statements. It is most suited to higher attaining infant children.

Skill Activity 30

Pupil activity: *How good is the explanation?*

Purpose

To think about what makes a good explanation.

What to do

This activity would be best carried out when the children are working on electric circuits. If working in other areas make up similar statements for them to evaluate. Tell the children that they have a chance to be teachers and to mark other children's work. Explain that all the children have tried to write an explanation but that some are better than others. They have to write what they think of the explanations in the box on the worksheet. Ask them to work in pairs and tell them that they should be able to tell you what they did, or did not, like about each explanation.

Possible responses would be:

Explanation	Mark	Comment
The bulb does not light up because it cannot.	Bad	Does not tell you anything new.
The bulb does not light up because both wires go to the same end of the battery.	Good	Explains clearly why the circuit does not work.
The bulb does not light up because it needs another wire.	OK	Tells you that it is something to do with the wiring but does not say that the wire needs to go to the other end of the battery.
The bulb lights up because it has two wires.	OK	Explains that two wires are needed to make this circuit complete but not that they have to be part of a circuit.
The bulb lights up because we got it right.	Bad	Does not explain what was right about the circuit.
The bulb lights up because it is in a circuit and the electricity has to go through the bulb.	Good	Explains that the bulb has to be part of a circuit to make it light up.

ıme ....

ow good is the explanation?

ome children made electric circuits. Some of the circuits made the
ılb light up. Some of them did not. Their teacher asked them to
:plain what happened.

ıy how well they explained. Write ⎡ Good ⎤, ⎡ OK ⎤ or ⎡ Bad ⎤
 the boxes.

ircuit 1

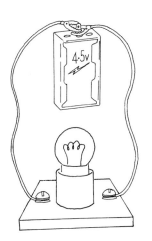

The bulb does not light up
because it cannot.

The bulb does not light up
because both wires go to the
same end of the battery.

The bulb does not light up
because it needs another wire.

ircuit 2

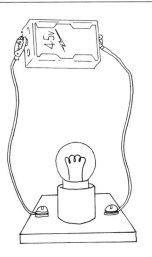

The bulb lights up because
it has two wires.

The bulb lights up because
we got it right.

The bulb lights up because it
is in a circuit and the electricity
has to go through the bulb.